Coloring Book For Adults Relaxation

Adult Coloring Book Creative Haven Magical Fairies Coloring Book : Fairy and Fantasy Grayscale Coloring Book (Stress Relief)

ISBN: 9798551691136

Copyright 2020 © Crazy Craft

All Right Reserved.

Copyright 2020 © Crazy Craft

All Right Reserved.

All rights reserved. No part of this publication may be reproduced or used in any from or by any means- graphic, electronic, mechanical, including photocopying,recording, or information stroage and retrival without permission of the publisher.

The designs in this book are intended for the personal, noncommercial use of the retail purchaser and are under federal copyright laws; they are not to be reprodeced in any from for commercial use. Permission is granted to photocopy content for the personal use of the retail purchaser.

COLORING BOOK

Have question ? Let us know.
crazycraftcoloringbook@gmail.com

 /crazycraftcoloringbook    @crazycraftcoloringbook

www.ingramcontent.com/pod-product-compliance
Lightning Source LLC
LaVergne TN
LVHW082242020125
800430LV00039B/1613